THE COMPLETE LOW-CARB COOKBOOK

THE BEST HOMEMADE RECIPES FOR A LOW-CARB LIFESTYLE

SPIKE KIMMONS

TABLE OF CONTENTS:

CHAPTER 1: BREAKFAST RECIPES 6
- LOW-CARB KETO BREAKFAST MUFFINS 7
- LOW-CARB CHEESECAKE 9
- SAVORY BREAKFAST CREPES 12
- PANCAKE CREPES 14
- YELLOW CAKE 16
- WHIPPED CAULIFLOWER, LOW-CARB 18
- CREAM CHEESE PANCAKES 20
- ALMOND SHORTBREAD COOKIES 22
- PANCAKES WITH COCONUT FLOUR 24
- PEANUT BUTTER COOKIES 26
- BACON SPINACH EGG CUPS 28

CHAPTER 2: LUNCH RECIPES 31
- ZUCCHINI LASAGNA 32
- LAMB BURGERS 35
- ZUPPA TOSCANA 37
- ZUCCHINI PASTA 39
- SCRAMBLED CAULIFLOWER 41
- SALISBURY STEAK 43
- AMAZING LOW CARB CARBONARA 46
- CHICKEN NACHO BITES 48
- LOW-CARB MEATLOAF WITH PORK RINDS 50
- CHICKEN AND MUSHROOM SOUP 52
- BEEF CABBAGE STEW 54
- TURKEY QUINOA LASAGNA 56
- YELLOW SQUASH CASSEROLE 58
- CHICKEN CHILI CASSEROLE 60
- TUNA AND MACKEREL CAKES 62
- SHRIMP ENCHILADAS 64

CHAPTER 3: DINNER RECIPES 67
- ZUCCHINI PIZZA CASSEROLE 68
- SPICY TURKEY SOUP WITH CAULIFLOWER RICE 71
- VEGAN SPAGHETTI SQUASH BOLOGNESE 73

GRAIN-FREE BACON AND MUSHROOM RISOTTO	75
FAUX POTATO SOUP	77
LOW-CARB, LOW-FAT TURKEY GOULASH	79
CAULIFLOWER MOCK POTATO SALAD	81
KETO MEATBALLS	83
HAM AND CHEESE PINWHEELS	85
BUFFALO CHICKEN STUFFED MUSHROOMS	87
ZUCCHINI ENCHILADAS	89
TWICE-BAKED CAULIFLOWER CASSEROLE	91
LOW-CARB SALMON PATTIES WITH FRESH DILL	93

CHAPTER 4: SNACK & APPETIZER RECIPES 96

LOW-CARB TACOS	97
LOW-CARB KETO BREAD	99
ZUCCHINI CHIPS	101
QUINOA MUFFINS	103
STUFFED PEPPERS	105
KETO CHEESE TACO SHELLS	107
HOT DOG AND DIPPING SAUCE	109

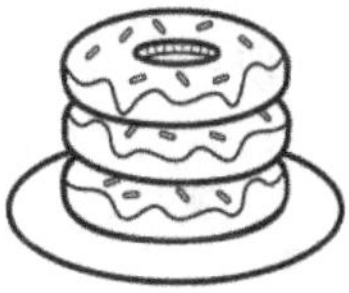

© Copyright 2021 by Spike Kimmons   All rights reserved.

The following Book is reproduced below with the goal of providing information that is as accurate and reliable as possible. Regardless, purchasing this Book can be seen as consent to the fact that both the publisher and the author of this book are in no way experts on the topics discussed within and that any recommendations or suggestions that are made herein are for entertainment

purposes only. Professionals

should be consulted as needed prior to undertaking any of the action endorsed herein.

This declaration is deemed fair and valid by both the American Bar Association and the Committee of Publishers Association and is legally binding throughout the United States.

Furthermore, the transmission, duplication, or reproduction of any of the following work including specific information will be considered an illegal act irrespective of if it is done electronically or in print. This extends to creating a secondary or tertiary copy of the work or a recorded copy and is only allowed with the express written consent from the Publisher. All additional right reserved.

The information in the following pages is broadly considered a truthful and accurate account of facts and as such, any inattention, use, or misuse of the information in question by the reader will render any resulting actions solely under their purview. There are no scenarios in which the publisher or the original author of this work can be in any fashion deemed liable for any hardship or damages that may befall them after undertaking information described herein.Additionally,

the information in the following

pages is intended only for informational

purposes and should thus

be thought of as universal.

As befitting its nature, it is presented without assurance

regarding its prolonged validity or interim quality.

Trademarks that are mentioned are done without written

consent and can in no way be considered an endorsement

from the trademark holder.

CHAPTER 1: BREAKFAST RECIPES

LOW-CARB KETO BREAKFAST MUFFINS

Prep:
10 **mins**
Cook:
30 **mins**
Additional:
10 **mins**
Total:
50 **mins**
Servings:
8
Yield:
8 **muffins**

INGREDIENTS:

4 **slices bacon, cooked and chopped**
4 **eggs**
½ **cup salsa**
½ **cup almond flour**

DIRECTIONS:

1
Preheat the oven to 350 **degrees F** (175 **degrees C)**. **Grease** 8 muffin cups with cooking spray.

2
Blend bacon, eggs, salsa, and almond flour together in a blender on medium speed until thoroughly combined, about 30 seconds.

3
Pour mixture into prepared muffin cups.

4
Bake in the preheated oven until a toothpick inserted into the center of a muffin comes out clean, about 30 minutes. Let cool 10 minutes before serving.

NUTRITION FACTS:

110 **calories**; protein 6.7g; **carbohydrates** 2.9g; **fat** 8.2g; **cholesterol** 97.9mg; **sodium** 236.1mg.

LOW-CARB CHEESECAKE

Prep:
15 mins
Cook:
45 mins
Additional:
4 hrs 10 mins
Total:
4 hrs 70 mins
Servings:
16
Yield:
1 9-inch cheesecake

INGREDIENTS:

FOR THE CRUST:

- 2 cups blanched almond flour
- ⅓ cup butter, melted
- 3 tablespoons powdered erythritol sweetener
- 1 teaspoon vanilla extract

FOR THE FILLING:

- 4 (8 ounce) packages cream cheese, softened
- 1 ¼ cups powdered erythritol sweetener
- 3 large eggs
- 1 tablespoon lemon juice
- 1 teaspoon vanilla extract
- ¼ teaspoon lemon zest

DIRECTIONS:

1
Preheat the oven to 350 degrees F (175 degrees C). Grease a 9-inch springform pan. Line the bottom with parchment paper. Wrap the bottom and sides of the pan with aluminum foil if worried about leakage.

2
Stir almond flour, butter, erythritol, and vanilla extract together in a small bowl until well combined; the mixture will be crumbly. Press into the prepared pan bottom.

3
Bake on the center rack until in the preheated oven until just golden, 10 to 12 minutes. Allow to cool for 10 minutes.

4
Meanwhile, beat cream cheese and powdered sweetener together using an electric stand or hand mixer at low speed until fluffy. Beat in eggs, 1 at a time. Add lemon juice, vanilla extract, and lemon zest. Beat until well combined.

5
Bake on the center rack in the preheated oven until center is almost set and slightly jiggly in the center, 45 to 55 minutes.

6
Remove from the oven and let cool in the pan. Keep in the pan, cover, and refrigerate to fully set, at least 4 hours, to overnight. Run a knife gently around the sides to remove, unclamp, and carefully remove the pan; it should come right off.

NUTRITION FACTS:

335 **calories;** **protein** 8.7g; **carbohydrates** 22.1g; **fat** 32g; **cholesterol** 106.6mg; **sodium** 206.2mg.

SAVORY BREAKFAST CREPES

Prep:
25 mins
Cook:
20 mins
Total:
45 mins
Servings:
2
Yield:
2 servings

INGREDIENTS:

CREPES:

2 ounces cream cheese, softened
2 eggs
⅓ cup almond flour
1 tablespoon almond milk

EGGS:

¼ cup diced yellow bell pepper
1 tablespoon diced onion
½ cup packed baby spinach leaves
2 mushrooms, sliced
2 eggs, beaten
1 pinch salt and ground black pepper
1 tablespoon grated Cheddar cheese

DIRECTIONS:

1
Combine cream cheese, eggs, almond flour, and almond milk in a blender. Blend until smooth, 30 seconds to 1 minute.

2
Heat an 8-inch nonstick skillet over medium heat for about 2 minutes. Pour in 3 tablespoons of crepe batter and swirl until it covers the bottom of the skillet. Cook until lightly browned, about 1 minute per side. Transfer to a plate to cool and cover with parchment paper or a paper towel. Repeat until you have cooked 4 crepes.

3
Cook pepper and onion in the same skillet until onions are translucent, about 3 minutes. Add spinach and mushrooms and cook until spinach is slightly wilted, 2 to 3 minutes. Add eggs; season with salt and pepper. Scramble until eggs reach desired consistency, about 2 minutes. Top with Cheddar cheese.

4
To assemble the crepe: Place scrambled egg mixture down the center of 2 crepes and fold over from each side. Reserve remaining crepes for later use.

NUTRITION FACTS:

386 calories; protein 20.4g; carbohydrates 8.7g; fat 31.1g; cholesterol 385.2mg; sodium 331.2mg.

PANCAKE CREPES

Prep:
5 mins
Cook:
20 mins
Total:
25 mins

INGREDIENTS:

3 ounces cream cheese, softened
2 eggs, beaten
1 teaspoon ground cinnamon
1 tablespoon sugar-free syrup
1 teaspoon butter

DIRECTIONS:

1
In a bowl, mash the cream cheese with beaten eggs, about 1 teaspoon at a time at first, until the mixture is smooth and free of lumps. Beat in the cinnamon and sugar-free syrup.

2
Melt the butter in a nonstick skillet over medium heat. When the butter has stopped foaming, reduce heat to medium-low, and pour in several tablespoons of the batter. Swirl to coat the bottom of the skillet. Allow to cook until set, about 4 minutes on the first side; flip the crepe with a spatula and cook the other side until the crepe shows small browned spots, 1 to 2 more minutes.

NUTRITION FACTS:

241 **calories;** **protein** 9.6g; **carbohydrates** 2.4g; **fat** 21.8g; **cholesterol** 238.2mg; **sodium** 215.4mg.

YELLOW CAKE

Prep:
15 **mins**
Cook:
20 **mins**
Total:
35 **mins**
Servings:
9
Yield:
1 8-**inch cake**

INGREDIENTS:

½ **cup butter**
½ **cup granular sucralose sweetener**
4 **egg yolks**
1 **teaspoon vanilla extract**
2 **teaspoons baking powder**
¼ **teaspoon salt**
1 **cup almond flour**
4 **teaspoons coconut flour**
¼ **cup heavy cream**

DIRECTIONS:

1
Preheat the oven to 350 degrees F (175 degrees C). Grease an 8x8-inch cake pan.

2
Combine butter and sucralose in a mixing bowl; beat with an electric mixer until creamy. Add egg yolks and vanilla extract and mix well. Add in baking powder and salt.

3
Mix almond flour and coconut flour into the creamed butter mixture. Pour in heavy cream and mix until combined. Pour batter into the prepared pan.

4
Bake in the preheated oven until a toothpick inserted into the center comes out clean, 20 to 25 minutes.

NUTRITION FACTS:

229 calories; protein 4.6g; carbohydrates 5.6g; fat 21.7g; cholesterol 127.2mg; sodium 251.7mg.

WHIPPED CAULIFLOWER, LOW-CARB

Prep:
10 mins
Cook:
10 mins
Total:
20 mins
Servings:
4
Yield:
4 servings

INGREDIENTS:

1 head cauliflower, cut into florets
¼ cup Parmesan cheese
1 tablespoon cream cheese at room temperature
2 teaspoons chicken soup base
2 teaspoons roasted garlic, or to taste
1 ½ teaspoons butter at room temperature
½ teaspoon milk, or to taste (**Optional**)
salt and ground black pepper to taste

DIRECTIONS:

1

Bring a pot of water to a boil. Cook cauliflower florets in the boiling water until they are extremely tender, about 10 minutes; drain in a colander. Put several paper towels on top of the cauliflower and use back of a big bowl to press down and squeeze as much liquid from the cauliflower as you can.

2

Mix Parmesan cheese, cream cheese, chicken soup base, roasted garlic, and butter in a bowl. Add cauliflower to the cheese mixture; beat with an electric hand mixer until creamy, about 3 minutes. Beat milk into the mixture until you get your desired texture. Season with salt and pepper.

NUTRITION FACTS:

91 **calories;** protein 5.6g; **carbohydrates** 8.9g; **fat** 4.6g; **cholesterol** 13.1mg; **sodium** 531.3mg

CREAM CHEESE PANCAKES

Prep:
5 **mins**
Cook:
3 **mins**
Additional:
2 **mins**
Total:
10 **mins**
Servings:
4
Yield:
4 6-**inch pancakes**

INGREDIENTS:

2 **eggs**
2 **ounces cream cheese, softened**
1 **packet stevia**
½ **teaspoon ground cinnamon**

DIRECTIONS:

1
Combine eggs, cream cheese, stevia, and cinnamon in a blender; blend until smooth. Let batter sit until bubbles settle, about 2 minutes.

2
Heat a large skillet over medium heat. Pour 1/4 of the batter onto the skillet; cook until golden brown, about 2 minutes. Flip and continue cooking until second side is golden brown, about 1 minute more. Repeat with remaining batter.

NUTRITION FACTS:

86 **calories;** **protein** 4.2g; **carbohydrates** 1g; **fat** 7.4g; **cholesterol** 108.6mg; **sodium** 77mg

ALMOND SHORTBREAD COOKIES

Prep:
15 mins
Cook:
15 mins
Additional:
15 mins
Total:
45 mins
Servings:
20
Yield:
20 small cookies

INGREDIENTS:

¾ **cup almond flour**
3 **tablespoons granular no-calorie sucralose sweetener**
1 **dash salt**
2 **tablespoons butter, softened**
1 **egg white**
¼ **teaspoon vanilla extract**

DIRECTIONS:

1
Mix almond flour, sweetener, and salt together in a small bowl with a fork. Add butter, egg white, and vanilla extract; continue mixing with a fork. Place in the freezer to help it harden for 15 minutes.

2
Meanwhile, preheat the oven to 325 degrees F (165 degrees C). Line a baking sheet with parchment paper or use a silicone baking mat.

3
Remove batter from freezer. Measure out 1 teaspoon at a time; roll into balls and place on the prepared baking sheet. Place plastic wrap on the bottom of a glass and roll dough balls flat.

4
Bake in the preheated oven until light, golden brown, 15 to 20 minutes.

NUTRITION FACTS:

39 calories; protein 1.2g; carbohydrates 1.2g; fat 3.5g; cholesterol 3.1mg; sodium 30.3mg.

PANCAKES WITH COCONUT FLOUR

Prep:
10 mins
Cook:
20 mins
Total:
30 mins
Servings:
6
Yield:
6 pancakes

INGREDIENTS:

- 1 teaspoon butter, or as needed
- 4 eggs
- ½ cup Greek yogurt
- ¼ cup water
- ¼ cup coconut flour
- 2 tablespoons coconut oil, melted
- 1 tablespoon flaxseed meal
- 2 teaspoons vanilla extract
- 2 teaspoons gluten-free baking powder
- 2 teaspoons ground cinnamon
- ½ teaspoon salt
- ½ teaspoon stevia powder

DIRECTIONS:

1
Heat a cast iron skillet over medium-low heat and grease with butter.

2
Whisk eggs, yogurt, water, coconut flour, coconut oil, flaxseed meal, vanilla extract, baking powder, cinnamon, salt, and stevia together in a large bowl.

3
Drop batter into the hot skillet using a 1/3 cup measuring cup. Cook until bubbles form and the pancakes are firm enough to flip, 4 to 5 minutes. Be sure to cook them on low enough heat that the outside doesn't burn before the inside is done. Flip and cook until browned on the other side and done in the middle, 2 to 3 minutes. Repeat with remaining batter

NUTRITION FACTS:

151 **calories**; **protein** 6.2g; **carbohydrates** 6.5g; **fat** 11.3g; **cholesterol** 129.5mg; **sodium** 419.5mg.

PEANUT BUTTER COOKIES

Prep:
10 **mins**
Cook:
12 **mins**
Total:
22 **mins**
Servings:
16
Yield:
16 **cookies**

INGREDIENTS:

1 **cup peanut butter**
1 **cup white sugar substitute**
1 **large egg**
1 **teaspoon vanilla extract**

DIRECTIONS:

1
Preheat oven to 350 **degrees F (**175 **degrees C). Line a baking sheet with a silicone baking mat.**

2
Mix peanut butter, sugar substitute, egg, and vanilla extract together in a bowl. Drop 16 **spoonfuls of dough** 1 **inch apart onto the prepared baking sheet.**

3
Bake in the preheated oven until set, about 12 **minutes.**

NUTRITION FACTS:

109 **calories;** **protein** 4.4g; **carbohydrates** 11.9g; **fat** 8.4g; **cholesterol** 11.6mg; **sodium** 78.4mg.

BACON SPINACH EGG CUPS

Prep:
15 **mins**
Cook:
40 **mins**
Additional:
5 **mins**
Total:
60 **mins**
Servings:
6
Yield:
12 **muffins**

INGREDIENTS:

cooking spray
4 **slices thick-cut bacon, diced**
½ (12 **ounce**) **package frozen chopped spinach, thawed and drained**
4 **mushrooms, chopped**
¼ **green bell pepper, chopped**
2 **slices onion, chopped**
1 **pinch salt and ground black pepper to taste**
6 **eggs**
1 **tablespoon heavy whipping cream**
1 ¼ **cups shredded Colby-Jack cheese, divided**
½ **teaspoon salt**
¼ **teaspoon ground black pepper**
1 **pinch onion powder**
1 **pinch garlic powder**

DIRECTIONS:

1
Preheat oven to 350 degrees F (175 degrees C). Spray 12 muffin cups with cooking spray.

2
Cook and stir bacon in a skillet over medium-high heat until crisp, about 10 minutes. Transfer bacon to a bowl, reserving bacon grease in the skillet.

3
Combine spinach, mushrooms, green bell pepper, onion, salt, and ground black pepper to taste in the skillet with bacon grease; cook and stir until softened, about 5 minutes. Transfer vegetable mixture to a bowl and place in the freezer to cool, about 5 minutes.

4
Whisk eggs and cream together in a bowl; stir in 1 cup Colby-Jack cheese, 1/2 teaspoon salt, 1/4 teaspoon ground black pepper, onion powder, and garlic powder. Add cooled vegetables and bacon to egg mixture and mix gently.

5
Scoop 1/4 cup egg mixture into each muffin cup; top each with remaining Colby-Jack cheese.

6
Bake in the preheated oven until egg cups are set, about 20 minutes.

NUTRITION FACTS:

237 calories; protein 16.5g; carbohydrates 4g; fat 17.7g; cholesterol 223.2mg; sodium 669mg.

CHAPTER 2: LUNCH RECIPES

ZUCCHINI LASAGNA

Prep:
20 mins
Cook:
1 hr 15 mins
Total:
1 hr 35 mins
Servings:
12
Yield:
1 9x13-inch lasagna

INGREDIENTS:

1 pound ground beef
1 pound bulk Italian sausage
½ cup diced onion
1 (26 ounce) jar pasta sauce
½ cup chicken broth
cooking spray
1 (16 ounce) container ricotta cheese
½ cup grated Parmesan cheese
2 eggs, beaten
1 tablespoon dried basil
4 medium zucchini, peeled
1 (8 ounce) package shredded mozzarella cheese

DIRECTIONS:

1

Heat a large nonstick skillet over medium-high heat. Cook and stir ground beef and Italian sausage in the hot skillet until browned and crumbly, 5 to 7 minutes. Add onion and saute until beginning to soften, about 3 minutes. Add pasta sauce and chicken broth. Bring to a simmer and cook, stirring occasionally, for 15 minutes.

2

Meanwhile, preheat the oven to 350 degrees F (175 degrees C). Spray a 9x13-inch baking pan with cooking spray.

3

Mix ricotta cheese, Parmesan cheese, eggs, and basil together in a small bowl.

4

Cut zucchini lengthwise into thin strips (1/8 inch to 1/4 inch thick) with a thin, sharp knife. Place a layer of tightly arranged zucchini slices in the prepared baking pan and spread a layer of the ricotta mixture on top. Top with a small amount of the meat sauce followed by 1 to 2 ounces of mozzarella cheese. Be sure not to overapply the sauce so you'll have enough for the very top of the dish.

5

Continue layering the lasagna
with zucchini slices,
ricotta mixture, meat sauce, and mozzarella.
Finish with a top layer of zucchini,
the remaining meat sauce,
and the remaining mozzarella.

6
Bake, uncovered, until sauce is bubbling and cheese is melted, 45 minutes to 1 hour. Drain any excess liquid from the edges of the baking pan with a baster or ladle during the last 30 minutes of cooking.

7
Cut portions with a sharp knife first and then carefully remove with a large spatula to serve.

NUTRITION FACTS:

359 **calories**; **protein** 24.5g; **carbohydrates** 15.1g; **fat** 22.1g; **cholesterol** 97.4mg; **sodium** 866mg.

LAMB BURGERS

Prep:
5 mins
Cook:
10 mins
Total:
15 mins
Servings:
4
Yield:
4 servings

INGREDIENTS:

1 **pound ground lamb**
1 **tablespoon soy sauce**
⅓ **cup chopped onion**
salt and ground black pepper to taste
⅛ **cup avocado oil**
⅓ **cup crumbled feta cheese (Optional)**

DIRECTIONS:

1
Put lamb, soy sauce, and onion in a bowl and season with salt and pepper to taste. Mix with hands to combine. Form lamb mixture into 4 patties.

2
Heat avocado oil in a skillet over medium heat. Cook lamb patties until browned, 5 to 8 minutes on each side. An instant-read meat thermometer, inserted into the center of a patty, should read at least 145 degrees F (65 degrees C). Sprinkle with feta cheese and serve.

NUTRITION FACTS:

296 **calories**; **protein** 22.9g; **carbohydrates** 3.1g; **fat** 20.9g; **cholesterol** 94.6mg; **sodium** 524.3mg.

ZUPPA TOSCANA

Prep:
20 mins
Cook:
43 mins
Total:
63 mins
Servings:
6
Yield:
6 servings

INGREDIENTS:

- 1 pound Italian sausage, casings removed
- 6 slices bacon, cut into 1/2-inch pieces
- 1 onion, diced
- 3 cloves garlic, pressed
- 2 (32 ounce) cartons chicken broth
- ½ cup water
- 1 cube chicken bouillon (such as Knorr®)
- 1 teaspoon ground black pepper
- 5 cups chopped cauliflower florets
- 3 cups stemmed and chopped kale
- ½ cup half-and-half
- ¼ cup grated Parmesan cheese

DIRECTIONS:

1
Cook the Italian sausage in a large pot over medium-high heat until browned and crumbly, 5 to 7 minutes. Drain off grease and transfer sausage to a plate.

2
Cook bacon to the same pot until crisp, 3 to 5 minutes. Remove and drain, leaving about 2 teaspoons of bacon grease in the pot. Add onion and garlic and cook until soft and translucent, about 5 minutes.

3
Return sausage and bacon back into the pot; stir in chicken broth, water, and bouillon cube. Season with pepper and simmer over low heat for 20 minutes. Stir in cauliflower and simmer until almost tender, about 5 minutes. Add kale and half-and-half; simmer until kale is wilted, about 5 minutes. Sprinkle with Parmesan cheese to serve.

NUTRITION FACTS:

349 **calories**; protein 20.2g; **carbohydrates** 17.1g; fat 22.5g; **cholesterol** 57.8mg; **sodium** 2564.4mg

ZUCCHINI PASTA

Prep:
10 **mins**
Cook:
5 **mins**
Total:
15 **mins**
Servings:
1
Yield:
1 **serving**

INGREDIENTS:

2 **zucchinis, peeled**
1 **tablespoon olive oil**
¼ **cup water**
salt and ground black pepper to taste

DIRECTIONS:

1
Cut lengthwise slices from zucchini using a vegetable peeler, stopping when the seeds are reached. Turn zucchini over and continue 'peeling' until all the zucchini is in long strips; discard seeds. Slice the zucchini into thinner strips resembling spaghetti.

2
Heat olive oil in a skillet over medium heat; cook and stir zucchini in the hot oil for 1 minute. Add water and cook until zucchini is softened, 5 to 7 minutes. Season with salt and pepper.

NUTRITION FACTS:

157 **calories**; **protein** 2.9g; **carbohydrates** 7.9g; **fat** 13.9g; **sodium** 180.7mg.

SCRAMBLED CAULIFLOWER

Prep:
15 **mins**
Cook:
25 **mins**
Total:
40 **mins**
Servings:
6
Yield:
6 **servings**

INGREDIENTS:

- 1 **head cauliflower, cut into florets**
- ½ **cup shredded Cheddar cheese**
- ½ **cup grated Parmesan cheese**
- 2 **large eggs, beaten**
- ½ **teaspoon cayenne pepper, or to taste**
- ¼ **teaspoon salt, or to taste**
- 2 **tablespoons butter**

DIRECTIONS:

1
Place cauliflower into a large pot and cover with water; bring to a boil. Reduce heat to medium-low and simmer until tender, 7 to 10 minutes. Drain.

2
Mash cauliflower in a bowl until smooth. Beat Cheddar cheese, Parmesan cheese, eggs, cayenne pepper, and salt into cauliflower.

3
Melt butter in a skillet over medium-high heat. Pour cauliflower mixture into hot butter and cook until golden, about 5 minutes. Flip cauliflower mixture; cook and stir until mixture is more crumbly than creamy, about 10 minutes more.

NUTRITION FACTS:

149 **calories;** protein 9g; **carbohydrates** 5.7g; **fat** 10.6g;

SALISBURY STEAK

Prep:
10 mins
Cook:
39 mins
Total:
49 mins

INGREDIENTS:

SALISBURY STEAKS:

- 2 pounds ground beef
- 1 onion, diced
- 2 eggs
- 1 tablespoon Worcestershire sauce
- 1 tablespoon dried parsley flakes
- 2 teaspoons salt
- ½ teaspoon garlic powder
- ½ teaspoon onion powder (Optional)
- ½ teaspoon ground black pepper

GRAVY:

- 7 tablespoons butter
- 2 cups sliced button mushrooms, or more to taste
- 1 tablespoon all-purpose flour
- 1 cup beef broth
- 1 teaspoon Worcestershire sauce
- ½ cup sour cream
- salt and ground black pepper to taste

DIRECTIONS:

1

Mix ground beef, onion, eggs, 1 tablespoon Worcestershire sauce, parsley, 2 teaspoons salt, garlic powder, onion powder, and 1/2 teaspoon pepper together in a bowl. Split steak mixture into 6 portions and form into patties.

2

Heat a large skillet over medium-high heat. Cook patties, 3 at a time, until slightly browned on one side, about 5 minutes. Flip and cook until other side is browned, about 5 minutes more. Repeat with remaining patties, pouring off any excess liquid. Place Salisbury steaks on a plate and cover with aluminum foil to maintain heat.

3

Melt butter in the same skillet over medium heat. Add mushrooms and cook until golden brown, about 5 minutes. Transfer mushrooms to a bowl, reserving butter in the skillet.

4

Stir flour into the butter until dissolved. Pour in beef broth slowly, stirring until thickened, about 7 minutes. Add 1 teaspoon Worcestershire sauce; cook, stirring frequently, until gravy starts to thicken slightly, about 5 minutes. Add sour cream and season with salt and pepper. Cook, stirring until all sour cream is melted and gravy is light brown, about 2 minutes.

5

Stir mushrooms back into the gravy. Remove from heat and let cool until thickened, about 2 minutes. Ladle gravy and mushrooms over steak patties.

NUTRITION FACTS:

536 **calories**; **protein** 29.7g; **carbohydrates** 7.5g; **fat** 42.9g; **cholesterol** 198.9mg; **sodium** 1190mg.

AMAZING LOW CARB CARBONARA

Prep:
15 mins
Cook:
1 hr 15 mins
Total:
1 hr 30 mins
Servings:
12
Yield:
1 9x13-inch casserole dish

INGREDIENTS:

1 spaghetti squash, halved and seeded
6 eggs
1 (12 fluid ounce) can evaporated milk
1 tablespoon garlic powder
1 tablespoon salt
1 tablespoon dried oregano
1 pound chopped cooked chicken
14 ounces shredded Parmesan cheese, divided
1 bunch green onions, chopped, divided
¼ cup bacon bits
ground black pepper to taste

DIRECTIONS:

1
Preheat oven to 375 degrees F (190 degrees C). Line a baking sheet with parchment paper.

2
Place squash, cut-side down, onto prepared baking sheet.

3
Bake in the preheated oven until flesh is tender, 30 to 45 minutes. Cool until easily handled.

4
Scrape spaghetti squash flesh into a large bowl using a fork. Whisk eggs, evaporated milk, garlic powder, salt, and oregano together in a separate bowl; pour over squash. Mix chicken, 1/2 of the Parmesan cheese, 1/2 of the green onions, bacon bits, and black pepper into squash mixture; pour into a 9x13-inch casserole dish. Top mixture with remaining Parmesan cheese and green onions.

5
Bake in the oven until cooked through and set, about 45 minutes.

NUTRITION FACTS:

326 calories; protein 30.3g; carbohydrates 10.9g; fat 18.1g; cholesterol 161.3mg;

CHICKEN NACHO BITES

Prep:
20 **mins**
Cook:
15 **mins**
Total:
35 **mins**
Servings:
4
Yield:
4 **servings**

INGREDIENTS:

1 **large cooked chicken breast, shredded**
1 **cup pico de gallo, divided**
1 **cup sour cream, divided**
1 **cup shredded Mexican cheese blend**
1 **tablespoon taco seasoning mix**
cooking spray
1 (8 **ounce) package mini sweet bell peppers, halved lengthwise and seeded**
1 (2.25 **ounce) can chopped olives**

DIRECTIONS:

1
Preheat oven to 350 **degrees F (**175 **degrees C).**

2
Combine shredded chicken, 1/2 **cup pico de gallo,** 1/2 **cup sour cream,** 1/2 **cup Mexican cheese blend, and taco seasoning in a large bowl.**

3
Spray a baking dish with cooking spray. Fill each pepper with as much chicken mixture as possible and place in the baking dish. Sprinkle pepper halves with 1/4 **cup Mexican cheese blend. Cover with olives and remaining** 1/4 **cup cheese.**

4
Bake in the preheated oven until cheese is melted and peppers have begun to soften, 15 **to** 20 **minutes. Top each cooked pepper with a dollop of pico de gallo and sour cream.**

NUTRITION FACTS:

388 **calories; protein** 23.3g**; carbohydrates** 11.7g**; fat** 26.1g**; cholesterol** 93.7mg**; sodium** 933.6mg**.**

LOW-CARB MEATLOAF WITH PORK RINDS

Prep:
15 mins
Cook:
1 hr
Total:
1 hr 15 mins
Servings:
6
Yield:
1 meatloaf

INGREDIENTS:

1 ½ **pounds ground beef**
1 **cup crushed pork rinds**
½ **cup grated Parmesan cheese**
⅓ **cup tomato sauce**
¼ **cup chopped onion**
1 **large egg**
2 **tablespoons chopped fresh parsley**
½ **teaspoon salt**
½ **teaspoon ground black pepper**
½ **teaspoon garlic powder**

DIRECTIONS:

1
Preheat the oven to 350 degrees F (175 degrees C). Lightly grease a 9x5-inch loaf pan.

2
Combine beef, pork rinds, Parmesan cheese, tomato sauce, onion, egg, parsley, salt, pepper, and garlic powder in a bowl and shape into a loaf. Transfer to the prepared pan.

3
Bake in the preheated oven until browned and no longer pink in the center, about 1 hour. An instant-read thermometer inserted into the center should read at least 160 degrees F (70 degrees C).

NUTRITION FACTS:

470 **calories**; protein 44.7g; **carbohydrates** 2.1g; **fat** 32.7g; cholesterol 161.9mg; **sodium** 715.2mg.

CHICKEN AND MUSHROOM SOUP

Prep:
20 **mins**
Cook:
38 **mins**
Total:
58 **mins**
Servings:
6
Yield:
6 servings

INGREDIENTS:

½ **cup butter**
1 **cooked chicken breast, cubed**
1 **small white onion, finely chopped**
3 **cloves garlic, finely chopped**
1 ½ **pounds fresh mushrooms, sliced**
3 **cups chicken stock**
3 **tablespoons chopped fresh tarragon, divided**
salt and freshly ground black pepper to taste
2 **cups heavy whipping cream**

DIRECTIONS:

1
Melt butter in a Dutch oven over medium-high heat. Add chicken; saute until lightly browned, about 3 minutes. Add onion and garlic; saute until softened, about 5 minutes. Stir in mushrooms; saute until tender, 5 to 10 minutes. Pour in chicken stock and 2 tablespoons tarragon; reduce heat to low. Season with salt. Cover and simmer soup until flavors are combined, about 25 minutes.

2
Stir cream into the soup; cook until heated through but not boiling. Serve soup with pepper and the remaining tarragon on top.

NUTRITION FACTS:

531 **calories**; protein 15.3g; **carbohydrates** 8.2g; **fat** 50.2g; **cholesterol** 179.2mg; **sodium** 539.8mg

BEEF CABBAGE STEW

Prep:
15 mins
Cook:
2 hrs 5 mins
Total:
2 hrs 20 mins
Servings:
8
Yield:
8 servings

INGREDIENTS:

2 pounds beef stew meat, trimmed and cut into 1-inch cubes
1 cube beef bouillon
1 ⅓ cups hot chicken broth
2 large onions, coarsely chopped
1 teaspoon Greek seasoning
¼ teaspoon ground black pepper
2 bay leaves
1 (8 ounce) package shredded cabbage
5 stalks celery, sliced
1 (8 ounce) can whole plum tomatoes, coarsely chopped
1 (8 ounce) can tomato sauce
salt to taste

DIRECTIONS:

1
Cook and stir beef in a large saucepan or Dutch oven until browned, about 5 minutes; drain excess grease.

2
Stir beef bouillon into chicken broth in a bowl until dissolved; add to beef.

3
Mix onions, Greek seasoning, black pepper, and bay leaves into broth-beef mixture; cover saucepan and simmer until beef is tender, about 1 hour 15 minutes. Add cabbage and celery to broth-beef mixture; cover saucepan and simmer until celery is tender, about 30 minutes more.

4
Stir plum tomatoes, tomato sauce, and salt into broth-beef mixture and simmer, uncovered, until stew is slightly thickened, 15 to 20 minutes. Remove and discard bay leaves before serving.

NUTRITION FACTS:

372 **calories**; **protein** 31.8g; **carbohydrates** 9g; **fat** 22.7g; **cholesterol** 99.5mg; **sodium** 612.1mg

TURKEY QUINOA LASAGNA

Prep:
20 mins
Cook:
1 hr 20 mins
Total:
1 hr 40 mins
Servings:
12
Yield:
1 9x13-inch baking pan

INGREDIENTS:

¼ cup olive oil, divided
2 eggplants, peeled and sliced 1/8-inch thick
3 cloves garlic, minced
1 pound ground turkey
1 small yellow onion, chopped
1 cup quinoa
salt and ground black pepper to taste
1 (24 ounce) jar spaghetti sauce
1 (16 ounce) package shredded mozzarella cheese
1 (16 ounce) package shredded Cheddar-Monterey Jack cheese blend
1 tablespoon Parmesan cheese (Optional)

DIRECTIONS:

1
Heat 1 tablespoon oil in a large skillet over medium-high heat. Fry eggplant slices a single layer at a time, replenishing oil between batches, until golden brown and soft, about 1 minute per side.

2
Preheat oven to 350 degrees F (175 degrees C).

3
Heat remaining 1 tablespoon olive oil in the skillet over medium heat. Add garlic; cook and stir until fragrant, about 1 minute. Add turkey and onion; cook and stir until turkey is crumbled and no longer pink, about 5 minutes. Stir in quinoa and season with salt and pepper. Pour in spaghetti sauce; cook until sauce is bubbly, 5 to 10 minutes.

4
Spread a layer of sauce in the bottom of a 9x13-inch baking pan. Top with even layers of eggplant slices and Cheddar-Monterey Jack cheese. Repeat layering sauce, eggplant, and cheese, ending with sauce on top. Spread mozzarella cheese evenly on top. Cover with aluminum foil.

5
Bake in the preheated oven until cheese is melted and bubbly, about 45 minutes. Uncover and continue baking until top is golden, about 15 minutes more.

NUTRITION FACTS:

465 **calories;** protein 29.6g; **carbohydrates** 25.3g; **fat** 27.7g;

YELLOW SQUASH CASSEROLE

Prep:
20 **mins**
Cook:
35 **mins**
Total:
55 **mins**
Servings:
8
Yield:
8 **servings**

INGREDIENTS:

1 **tablespoon olive oil**
1 **teaspoon butter**
1 **small onion, chopped**
2 **cloves garlic, minced**
4 **cups peeled and cubed yellow squash**
1 **teaspoon kosher salt**
½ **teaspoon freshly ground black pepper**
⅓ **cup finely chopped raw almonds**
1 **cup shredded Colby-Monterey Jack cheese, divided**
½ **cup heavy whipping cream**
2 **eggs**
⅓ **cup coarsely chopped roasted, salted almonds**

DIRECTIONS:

1
Preheat oven to 400 **degrees F** (200 **degrees C**).

2
Heat olive oil and butter in a skillet over medium-high heat; cook and stir onion and garlic in the hot oil-butter mixture until softened, about 3 minutes. Add squash, salt, and pepper; stir to combine. Cover skillet and cook, stirring occasionally, until squash is softened, about 5 minutes. Transfer squash mixture to a large bowl.

3
Mix raw almonds and 1/2 cup Colby-Monterey Jack cheese together in a bowl; stir into squash mixture. Whisk cream and eggs together in a measuring cup or small bowl; stir into squash mixture. Pour squash mixture into a 9x13-inch casserole dish; top with remaining Colby-Monterey Jack cheese and roasted almonds.

4
Bake in the preheated oven until casserole is golden brown and bubbling, 25 to 30 **minutes**.

NUTRITION FACTS:

228 **calories**; protein 8.6g; **carbohydrates** 6.7g; fat 19.6g; **cholesterol** 84.6mg; **sodium** 418.8mg

CHICKEN CHILI CASSEROLE

Prep:
15 **mins**
Cook:
50 **mins**
Total:
65 **mins**
Servings:
6
Yield:
1 8-**inch casserole**

INGREDIENTS:

2 **tablespoons olive oil**
½ **cup diced onion**
1 **large cooked chicken breast, shredded**
1 ½ **teaspoons chili powder**
1 **teaspoon garlic powder**
1 **teaspoon ground black pepper**
½ **teaspoon seasoned salt**
½ **teaspoon red pepper flakes**
½ **teaspoon ground cumin**
1 **cup shredded Cheddar cheese**
2 (4 **ounce**) **cans diced green chiles**
¾ **cup milk**
2 **large eggs**
¼ **cup crushed pork rinds**

DIRECTIONS:

1
Preheat the oven to 375 degrees F (190 degrees C). Lightly grease an 8-inch square baking pan.

2
Heat oil in a skillet over medium heat; stir in onion. Cook and stir until the onion has softened and turned translucent, about 5 minutes.

3
Combine onion with shredded chicken, chili powder, garlic powder, black pepper, seasoned salt, red pepper flakes, and cumin. Stir in 1/2 cup Cheddar cheese and green chiles. Spread in the bottom of the prepared baking pan and top with remaining Cheddar.

4
Whisk milk and eggs together in a bowl. Stir in crushed pork rinds and pour over top of the casserole.

5
Bake, uncovered, in the preheated oven until top of casserole is set, about 45 minutes.

NUTRITION FACTS:

275 **calories**; **protein** 22.7g; **carbohydrates** 6.2g; **fat** 18.3g; **cholesterol** 121.8mg;

TUNA AND MACKEREL CAKES

Prep:
15 **mins**
Cook:
10 **mins**
Total:
25 **mins**
Servings:
8
Yield:
8 **servings**

INGREDIENTS:

1 (15 **ounce**) **can mackerel in brine, drained**
1 **small onion, chopped**
1 (5 **ounce**) **can tuna packed in water, drained**
¼ **cup grated Parmesan cheese**
¼ **cup mayonnaise**
2 **egg, beaten**
2 **tablespoons Dijon mustard**
2 **teaspoons salt-free seasoning blend**
1 **teaspoon paprika**
1 **teaspoon dried sweet basil**
1 (3.5 **ounce**) **bag pork rinds, crushed**
butter-flavored cooking spray

DIRECTIONS:

1

Mix mackerel, onion, tuna, Parmesan cheese, mayonnaise, eggs, Dijon mustard, seasoning blend, paprika, and basil together in a bowl. Add pork rind crumbs, 1 to 2 tablespoons at a time, until mixture holds together. Form mixture into balls and flatten into 1/2-inch-thick cakes.

2

Heat a large non-stick skillet over medium-high heat and grease with cooking spray. Arrange cakes in the hot skillet and spray each cake with cooking spray.

3

Cook cakes, working in batches if needed, in the hot skillet until browned, 3 to 5 minutes; gently flatten cakes with the back of a fork. Flip cakes and cook until other side is browned, 3 to 5 minutes. Transfer cakes to a paper towel-lined plate.

NUTRITION FACTS:

242 **calories;** protein 24.8g; **carbohydrates** 2.2g; **fat** 14.3g; cholesterol 103.3mg; **sodium** 593.1mg.

SHRIMP ENCHILADAS

Prep:
15 **mins**
Cook:
30 **mins**
Total:
45 **mins**
Servings:
5
Yield:
5 **servings**

INGREDIENTS:

1 **tablespoon extra-virgin olive oil**
20 **each uncooked medium shrimp, peeled and deveined**
1 **red bell pepper, chopped**
½ **sweet onion, chopped**
5 **each low-carb tortillas**
¼ **cup enchilada sauce**
⅓ **cup** 2% **milk shredded Cheddar cheese**
⅓ **cup** 2% **milk shredded mozzarella cheese**

DIRECTIONS:

1
Preheat the oven to 350 degrees F (175 degrees C).

2
Heat oil in a nonstick pan over medium-high heat. Cook and stir shrimp in the hot oil until pink, 3 to 4 minutes. Transfer to a bowl. Pour bell pepper and onion into the pan and cook until onion is translucent, about 5 minutes; add to the bowl with shrimp and set aside. Clean the pan.

3
Place tortillas, 1 at a time, into the pan and toast over medium-low heat until light brown, about 1 minute per tortilla.

4
Put 1/5 of the shrimp mixture down the center of each tortilla. Fold/roll up and place into a baking dish. Place 1 tablespoon of enchilada sauce on each; then sprinkle evenly with Cheddar and mozzarella cheeses.

5
Bake in the preheated oven until melted, about 15 minutes. Let cool slightly before serving.

NUTRITION FACTS:

172 **calories; protein** 17.3g; **carbohydrates** 15.1g; **fat** 8.4g; **cholesterol** 70.3mg; **sodium** 348.2mg.

CHAPTER 3: DINNER RECIPES

ZUCCHINI PIZZA CASSEROLE

Prep:
10 **mins**
Cook:
40 **mins**
Additional:
10 **mins**
Total:
60 **mins**
Servings:
8
Yield:
8 **servings**

INGREDIENTS:

4 **cups shredded zucchini**
¼ **teaspoon salt**
2 **large eggs**
1 ½ **cups shredded mozzarella cheese, divided**
½ **cup grated Parmesan cheese**
1 **teaspoon Italian seasoning**
½ **teaspoon garlic powder**
1 **pound** 85% **lean ground beef**
½ **white onion, chopped**
1 **cup pizza sauce**
1 **ounce pepperoni slices**

DIRECTIONS:

1

Preheat the oven to 400 degrees F (200 degrees C). Grease a 10x13-inch baking dish.

2

Place shredded zucchini in a colander and sprinkle salt on top. Press down to drain as much water as possible. Let sit for 10 minutes. Transfer to a large bowl.

3

Add eggs, 1/2 of the mozzarella cheese, Parmesan cheese, Italian seasoning, and garlic powder to the zucchini. Mix well. Press mixture into the prepared baking dish.

4

Bake uncovered in the preheated oven for 20 minutes.

5

Heat a large skillet over medium-high heat. Cook and stir ground beef and onion in the hot skillet until beef is browned and crumbly, 5 to 7 minutes. Drain and discard grease. Mix pizza sauce with cooked beef and spoon over zucchini mixture in the baking pan.

6

Sprinkle remaining mozzarella cheese over the meat. Top with pepperoni slices.

7

Return baking dish to the hot oven and bake until mozzarella cheese is melted, 15 to 20 minutes more.

NUTRITION FACTS:

255 **calories**; **protein** 21.8**g**; **carbohydrates** 6**g**; **fat** 15.6**g**; **cholesterol** 111.7**mg**; **sodium** 563.2**mg**.

SPICY TURKEY SOUP WITH CAULIFLOWER RICE

Prep:
30 **mins**
Cook:
1 **hr** 20 **mins**
Total:
1 **hr** 50 **mins**

INGREDIENTS:

- 4 **tablespoons butter, divided**
- 1 **pound pork sausage**
- 3 **stalks celery, chopped**
- 3 **carrots, chopped**
- 1 **onion, chopped**
- 1 **green bell pepper, chopped**
- 4 **cups chopped cooked turkey, or to taste**
- 1 (32 **fluid ounce) container chicken stock**
- 2 (10.75 **ounce) cans condensed cream of chicken soup (Optional)**
- 2 (10 **ounce) packages frozen riced cauliflower**
- 1 (10 **ounce) package frozen peas**
- 16 **ounces heavy cream**
- 1 **tablespoon Cajun seasoning**
- 2 **teaspoons ground thyme**
- 2 **teaspoons seasoned salt**
- 2 **teaspoons ground black pepper**
- 2 **teaspoons smoked paprika**
- 2 **teaspoons dried basil**
- 2 **teaspoons dried oregano**
- 1 **teaspoon red pepper flakes**
- 1 **teaspoon ground cayenne pepper**

DIRECTIONS:

1
Heat 2 tablespoons butter in a Dutch oven over medium-high heat. Brown sausage in the hot butter until browned and cooked through, 5 to 7 minutes. Transfer cooked sausage to a plate. Add celery, carrots, onion, bell pepper, and remaining butter to the pot. Cook over medium heat, scraping up browned bits and stirring to deglaze, 4 to 5 minutes.

2
Stir cooked sausage and turkey into the Dutch oven. Pour in chicken stock and cream of chicken soup. Stir and bring to a simmer, about 5 minutes. Add cauliflower rice and peas and return to a simmer, about 5 minutes. Stir in heavy cream, Cajun seasoning, thyme, seasoned salt, black pepper, smoked paprika, basil, oregano, red pepper flakes, and cayenne. Let simmer, stirring occasionally, for 1 hour. Season to taste and serve.

NUTRITION FACTS:

529 **calories;** protein 28.9g; **carbohydrates** 18.7g; **fat** 38.2g; **cholesterol** 148.2mg; **sodium** 1563.2mg.

VEGAN SPAGHETTI SQUASH BOLOGNESE

Prep:
15 **mins**
Cook:
10 **mins**
Total:
25 **mins**
Servings:
4
Yield:
4 **servings**

INGREDIENTS:

1 (3 **pound**) **spaghetti squash, halved and seeded**
1 **tablespoon olive oil**
½ **cup onion, chopped**
½ **pound vegetarian ground beef**
1 (15 **ounce**) **jar tomato sauce**
2 **tablespoons peanut butter**
1 **tablespoon dried oregano**
½ **teaspoon sweet paprika**
½ **teaspoon ground thyme**
½ **teaspoon tomato paste**
¼ **teaspoon ground turmeric**
salt and freshly ground pepper, to taste

DIRECTIONS:

1
Pierce spaghetti squash halves all over using a fork. Place in a microwave-safe dish and cook in a microwave oven until softened, about 10 minutes.

2
Meanwhile, heat oil in a saucepan over medium heat and cook onion until soft and translucent, about 4 minutes. Add vegetarian ground beef, tomato sauce, peanut butter, oregano, paprika, thyme, tomato paste, turmeric, salt, and pepper and mix well. Simmer until sauce is heated through and starts to thicken, 5 to 10 minutes.

3
Shred squash flesh using a fork and distribute among 4 plates. Serve with the sauce.

NUTRITION FACTS:

293 calories; protein 15.1g; carbohydrates 42g; fat 9.8g; sodium 892.5mg.

GRAIN-FREE BACON AND MUSHROOM RISOTTO

Prep:
15 mins
Cook:
18 mins
Total:
33 mins
Servings:
4
Yield:
4 servings

INGREDIENTS:

- ¼ **cup ghee**
- ½ **onion, finely chopped**
- 1 **clove garlic, minced**
- 2 **slices bacon, cut into small pieces**
- 1 **head cauliflower, grated**
- 1 **cup sliced fresh mushrooms**
- ½ **cup heavy whipping cream**
- 1 **cup grated Parmesan cheese**
- ½ **teaspoon salt**
- ¼ **teaspoon ground black pepper**
- ¼ **teaspoon ground nutmeg**

DIRECTIONS:

1
Melt ghee in a skillet over medium heat. Add onion and garlic; cook until tender, about 3 minutes. Add bacon and cook until evenly browned, about 4 minutes. Stir in grated cauliflower; cook for 3 minutes more. Add mushrooms and cook until tender, about 3 minutes.

2
Stir heavy cream, Parmesan cheese, salt, pepper, and nutmeg into the skillet; cook over medium heat until creamy, 5 to 7 minutes.

NUTRITION FACTS:

375 calories; protein 13.8g; carbohydrates 11.8g; fat 31.7g; cholesterol 96.1mg; sodium 757.1mg.

FAUX POTATO SOUP

Prep:
40 **mins**
Cook:
1 **hr** 5 **mins**
Total:
1 **hr** 45 **mins**
Servings:
10
Yield:
10 **servings**

INGREDIENTS:

3 **pounds turnips, peeled and cubed**
water to cover
2 **tablespoons olive oil, or more to taste**
4 **leeks, white portion only, thinly sliced**
4 **stalks celery, sliced**
4 **cups chicken stock, divided**
6 **strips cooked crispy bacon, or more to taste**
3 **tablespoons cornstarch**
2 **teaspoons salt, or to taste**
½ **teaspoon ground black pepper, or to taste**
2 **cups whole milk**
2 **green onions, sliced, or more to taste**

DIRECTIONS:

1
Place turnips in a pot and add water until covered by 3 to 4 inches; bring to a boil. Cook, stirring every 5 to 10 minutes, until soft, about 30 minutes. Drain.

2
Heat oil in the pot over medium heat. Add leeks and celery; cook and stir until slightly tender, about 5 minutes.

3
Blend leek mixture, 1 cup chicken stock, bacon, cornstarch, salt, and pepper in a food processor until smooth. Pour back into the pot.

4
Blend half of the turnips and 1 cup chicken stock in the food processor until smooth; pour into the pot. Repeat with remaining turnips and 1 cup chicken stock.

5
Pour remaining 1 cup chicken stock into the pot; stir in milk. Simmer, without boiling, until thickened, about 30 minutes. Ladle into bowls; garnish with green onions.

NUTRITION FACTS:

132 **calories;** protein 3.9g; **carbohydrates** 19.4g; **fat** 4.8g; **cholesterol** 6.9mg; **sodium** 983.4mg.

LOW-CARB, LOW-FAT TURKEY GOULASH

Prep:
15 mins
Cook:
32 mins
Total:
47 mins
Servings:
6
Yield:
6 cups

INGREDIENTS:

- 2 tablespoons olive oil
- 1 ¼ pounds ground turkey, or more to taste
- 2 yellow onions, diced
- 4 parsnips, diced
- 5 tablespoons paprika
- 1 clove garlic, chopped
- 1 teaspoon dried oregano
- salt to taste
- 3 cups chicken stock, or more as needed

DIRECTIONS:

1

Heat oil in a stockpot over medium heat. Add turkey; cook until browned and juices have cooked off, 5 to 7 minutes. Add onions; cook and stir until transparent, about 5 minutes. Add parsnips, paprika, garlic, and oregano. Cook, stirring frequently, until garlic is fragrant, about 2 minutes. Add chicken stock and a pinch of salt. Let simmer until thickened to desired consistency, 20 to 30 minutes.

NUTRITION FACTS:

232 **calories;** protein 20.8g; **carbohydrates** 11.1g; **fat** 12.8g; cholesterol 70.2mg; **sodium** 427.3mg.

CAULIFLOWER MOCK POTATO SALAD

Prep:
25 mins
Cook:
10 mins
Additional:
20 mins
Total:
55 mins
Servings:
8
Yield:
8 servings

INGREDIENTS:

4 quarts water
2 tablespoons salt
1 head cauliflower, cut into bite-sized pieces
1 cup mayonnaise
½ cup thinly sliced celery
3 slices cooked bacon, crumbled
4 tablespoons minced onion
3 tablespoons minced sweet pickles
1 teaspoon spicy mustard, or to taste
⅛ teaspoon ground turmeric
2 hard-boiled eggs, diced
salt and ground black pepper to taste

DIRECTIONS:

1

Bring water and salt to a boil over medium-high heat. Add cauliflower; bring back to a boil. Cook for 3 minutes. Remove from heat and drain.

2

Spread cauliflower pieces onto a metal tray and freeze until cool, 20 to 25 minutes.

3

Meanwhile, combine mayonnaise, celery, bacon, onion, pickles, mustard, and turmeric in a large bowl. Add cooled cauliflower and eggs; toss to combine. Season with salt and pepper.

NUTRITION FACTS:

242 **calories**; **protein** 3.4g; **carbohydrates** 6.3g; **fat** 23.3g; **cholesterol** 63.4mg; **sodium** 2000.7mg.

KETO MEATBALLS

Prep:
15 **mins**
Cook:
35 **mins**
Total:
50 **mins**
Servings:
6
Yield:
6 **servings**

INGREDIENTS:

1 ½ **pounds ground beef**
1 **egg**
2 **tablespoons grated Parmesan cheese**
1 **tablespoon flaxseed meal**
1 **teaspoon dried oregano**
salt and ground black pepper to taste
1 **tablespoon olive oil**
1 (14 **ounce) can tomato sauce**

DIRECTIONS:

1
Combine ground beef, egg, Parmesan cheese, flaxseed, oregano, salt, and pepper in a bowl; mix until well combined. Roll mixture into golf ball-size meatballs.

2
Heat olive oil in a large skillet over medium heat. Add meatballs; cook until browned, about 5 minutes on each side. Pour tomato sauce over meatballs; simmer for 25 to 30 minutes.

NUTRITION FACTS:

301 **calories;** protein 21.5g; **carbohydrates** 4.2g; **fat** 21.8g; **cholesterol** 102mg; **sodium** 475.7mg.

HAM AND CHEESE PINWHEELS

Prep:
20 **mins**
Additional:
1 **hr**
Total:
1 **hr** 20 **mins**
Servings:
14
Yield:
14 **servings**

INGREDIENTS:

- 1 (8 **ounce**) **package cream cheese, at room temperature**
- 3 **tablespoons horseradish sauce**
- 1 **tablespoon chopped fresh chives**
- 1 (8 **ounce**) **package thinly sliced ham**
- 1 (8 **ounce**) **package American cheese**

DIRECTIONS:

1

Combine cream cheese, horseradish, and chives in a small bowl.

2

Pat each ham slice dry with a paper towel and spread a thin layer of the cream cheese mixture on top. Place 1 slice American cheese over each; you may need more than 1 slice to cover the ham. Spread another thin layer of cream cheese mixture on top; roll into a pinwheel.

3

Cover pinwheels with plastic wrap and chill in the refrigerator until firm, 1 hour to overnight. Trim off ends with a sharp knife and slice each roll into 1/2-inch slices.

NUTRITION FACTS:

144 **calories**; **protein** 7.5g; **carbohydrates** 1.7g; **fat** 12g; **cholesterol** 41.8mg; **sodium** 504.3mg.

BUFFALO CHICKEN STUFFED MUSHROOMS

Prep:
15 **mins**
Cook:
30 **mins**
Total:
45 **mins**
Servings:
10
Yield:
10 **servings**

INGREDIENTS:

- 10 **large mushrooms, stems and insides removed**
- 1 **teaspoon olive oil, or as needed**
- 1 **celery stalk, diced**
- ¼ **cup blue cheese dressing**
- ¼ **cup ranch dressing**
- ¼ **cup buffalo wing sauce**
- 2 **ounces cream cheese**
- 2 **cooked chicken breasts, shredded**
- ½ **cup shredded Cheddar cheese**

DIRECTIONS:

1
Preheat oven to 350 **degrees F (**175 **degrees C).** Arrange mushrooms, open-side up, in a baking dish.

2
Heat olive oil in a small skillet over medium heat; cook and stir celery until tender, about 5 minutes. Add blue cheese dressing, ranch dressing, buffalo wing sauce, and cream cheese to celery; cook and stir until cream cheese is melted and buffalo sauce is smooth, about 5 minutes.

3
Mix chicken and buffalo sauce together in a bowl until chicken is coated; spoon into mushrooms. Sprinkle Cheddar cheese over buffalo sauce.

4
Bake in the preheated oven until cheese is melted and golden, about 20 minutes.

NUTRITION FACTS:

165 **calories;** protein 9g; **carbohydrates** 2.9g; **fat** 13g; **cholesterol** 32.4mg; **sodium** 356.1mg.

ZUCCHINI ENCHILADAS

Prep:
35 **mins**
Cook:
35 **mins**
Additional:
5 **mins**
Total:
75 **mins**
Servings:
8
Yield:
1 9x11-**inch baking dish**

INGREDIENTS:

1 **tablespoon olive oil**
1 **large onion, chopped**
kosher salt and ground black pepper to taste
1 **tablespoon ancho chile powder**
2 **cloves garlic, minced**
2 **teaspoons ground cumin**
1 **teaspoon sea salt**
2 **pounds cooked chicken breasts, shredded**
1 ½ **cups red enchilada sauce, divided**
2 **cups shredded sharp Cheddar cheese, divided**
4 **green onions, green and white parts chopped and separated**
¼ **cup chopped fresh cilantro**
4 **large zucchini, thinly sliced lengthwise**
½ **cup queso fresco, or more to taste**
¼ **cup sour cream (Optional)**
2 **tablespoons chopped fresh cilantro, or to taste**

DIRECTIONS:

1
Preheat the oven to 375 degrees F (190 degrees C).

2
Heat olive oil in a large skillet over medium heat. Saute onion until softened, about 5 minutes. Season with salt and pepper. Add chile powder, garlic, cumin, and sea salt; stir until combined. Add chicken and 1 cup enchilada sauce. Stir to combine and remove from heat. Let chicken mixture cool slightly.

3
Stir 1 cup Cheddar cheese, white parts of green onions, and 1/4 cup cilantro into the chicken mixture. Pour 1/4 cup enchilada sauce into the bottom of a 9x11-inch baking dish.

4
Slightly overlap 3 slices of zucchini on a cutting board. Top with a small mound of the chicken mixture. Roll up and place in the prepared baking dish. Repeat with remaining zucchini slices and chicken mixture. Spoon remaining 1/4 cup sauce over zucchini enchiladas. Sprinkle remaining 1 cup Cheddar cheese and queso fresco on top.

5
Bake in the preheated oven until cheese is melted, about 30 minutes. Garnish with green parts of green onions, sour cream, and 2 tablespoons cilantro.

NUTRITION FACTS:

478 calories; protein 48.8g; carbohydrates 11.7g; fat 26.3g; cholesterol 157.9mg;

TWICE-BAKED CAULIFLOWER CASSEROLE

Prep:
20 **mins**
Cook:
40 **mins**
Total:
60 **mins**
Servings:
6
Yield:
6 **servings**

INGREDIENTS:

1 **large head cauliflower, chopped**
1 ½ **cups shredded reduced-fat Cheddar cheese**
½ **cup bacon bits (such as Hormel®)**
½ **(8 ounce) package low-fat cream cheese**
½ **cup low-fat sour cream**
¼ **cup minced green onions**
3 **tablespoons butter**
salt and ground black pepper to taste

DIRECTIONS:

1

Preheat the oven to 350 degrees F (175 degrees C).

2

Bring a saucepan of water to a boil. Add cauliflower and cook until tender, but not overly soft, 3 to 5 minutes. Drain well and transfer cauliflower to a large bowl. Mash, using a potato masher, leaving some chunks.

3

Reserve 1/2 cup Cheddar cheese and 1 tablespoon bacon bits. Mix remaining Cheddar cheese, remaining bacon bits, cream cheese, sour cream, green onions, butter, salt, and pepper into the mashed cauliflower in the bowl. Transfer mixture to an 8-inch square baking dish. Sprinkle reserved Cheddar cheese and bacon bits on top.

4

Bake in the preheated oven until hot and bubbly, 30 to 35 minutes.

NUTRITION FACTS:

240 calories; protein 16.4g; carbohydrates 10.5g; fat 15.6g; cholesterol 46.3mg; sodium 639.9mg.

LOW-CARB SALMON PATTIES WITH FRESH DILL

Prep:
10 mins
Cook:
10 mins
Total:
20 mins
Servings:
4
Yield:
4 large patties

INGREDIENTS:

- 8 ounces cold baked salmon, broken into small pieces
- 2 eggs, beaten
- ⅓ cup almond meal
- 1 tablespoon chopped fresh dill
- ½ teaspoon onion powder
- ½ teaspoon lemon pepper
- ¼ teaspoon seafood seasoning
- ¼ teaspoon red pepper flakes
- 1 squeeze lemon juice
- ¼ cup butter

DIRECTIONS:

tep 1
Gently mix salmon, eggs, almond meal, dill, onion powder, lemon pepper, seafood seasoning, red pepper flakes, and lemon juice together in a bowl until well blended but not mushy; shape into 4 large patties.

2
Melt butter in a large skillet over medium heat. Fry patties in melted butter until browned completely, 5 to 7 minutes per side.

NUTRITION FACTS:

295 **calories**; **protein** 19.6g; **carbohydrates** 3.5g; **fat** 22.8g; **cholesterol** 159.3mg; **sodium** 242mg.

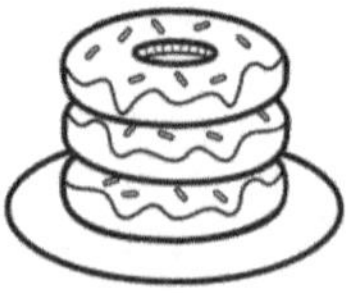

CHAPTER 4: SNACK & APPETIZER RECIPES

LOW-CARB TACOS

Prep:
20 **mins**
Cook:
15 **mins**
Total:
35 **mins**
Servings:
4
Yield:
4 **servings**

INGREDIENTS:

1 ½ **pounds ground beef**
1 **onion, diced**
½ (4 **ounce) can diced jalapeno peppers**
1 (1 **ounce) package taco seasoning mix**
2 **cups shredded lettuce**
1 **tomato, chopped**
½ **cup shredded reduced-fat Cheddar cheese**
¼ **cup salsa**
¼ **cup low-fat sour cream**
1 **avocado - peeled, pitted, and sliced**

DIRECTIONS:

1
Cook and stir ground beef, onion, and jalapeno peppers together in a skillet over medium-high heat until meat is browned and crumbly, 7 to 10 minutes. Stir taco seasoning into meat mixture; bring to a simmer and cook until flavors combine, about 5 minutes.

2
Stir meat mixture, shredded lettuce, tomato, Cheddar cheese, salsa, and sour cream together in a large bowl. Divide taco mixture among 4 bowls and top each with avocado slices.

NUTRITION FACTS:

521 **calories**; **protein** 34.9g; **carbohydrates** 16.3g; **fat** 34.9g; **cholesterol** 114.9mg; **sodium** 1061.9mg

LOW-CARB KETO BREAD

Prep:
15 **mins**
Cook:
40 **mins**
Additional:
15 **mins**
Total:
70 **mins**
Servings:
8
Yield:
1 **loaf**

INGREDIENTS:

olive oil cooking spray
⅔ **cup almond flour**
⅓ **cup coconut flour**
2 **teaspoons baking powder**
½ **teaspoon xanthan gum**
½ **teaspoon salt**
4 **eggs**
4 **egg whites**
¼ **cup butter, melted**
¼ **cup coconut oil, melted**
3 **tablespoons grapeseed oil**

DIRECTIONS:

1
Preheat oven to 350 degrees F (175 degrees C). Grease an 8x4-inch loaf pan with cooking spray.

2
Mix almond flour, coconut flour, baking powder, xanthan gum, and salt together in a large bowl.

3
Combine eggs and egg whites in a food processor; pulse until well beaten. Add almond flour mixture, butter, coconut oil, and grapeseed oil. Pulse until a smooth batter forms.

4
Spread batter in the prepared loaf pan.

5
Bake in the preheated oven until top is browned, about 40 minutes. Cool in the pan, about 15 minutes. Invert onto a cooling rack to finish cooling.

NUTRITION FACTS:

261 **calories;** protein 7.2g; **carbohydrates** 3.2g; **fat** 25.3g; **cholesterol** 108.3mg; **sodium** 378.1mg.

ZUCCHINI CHIPS

Prep:
10 **mins**
Cook:
2 **hrs**
Total:
2 **hrs** 10 **mins**
Servings:
2
Yield:
2 **servings**

INGREDIENTS:

2 **large large zucchini, thinly sliced**
1 **tablespoon olive oil, or to taste**
sea salt to taste

DIRECTIONS:

1
Preheat oven to 250 degrees F (120 degrees C).

2
Arrange sliced zucchini on a baking sheet. Drizzle lightly with olive oil and sprinkle lightly with sea salt.

3
Bake in the preheated oven until completely dried and chip-like, about 1 hour per side. Allow to cool before serving.

NUTRITION FACTS:

111 **calories**; **protein** 3.9g; **carbohydrates** 10.8g; **fat** 7.3g; **sodium** 192.4mg.

QUINOA MUFFINS

Prep:
15 mins
Cook:
20 mins
Total:
35 mins
Servings:
6
Yield:
6 muffins

INGREDIENTS:

cooking spray
1 cup cooked quinoa
3 large eggs, beaten
¼ cup crumbled feta cheese
¼ cup sliced mushrooms
¼ cup chopped onion
½ teaspoon dried thyme
salt and ground black pepper to taste

DIRECTIONS:

1
Preheat oven to 400 degrees F (200 degrees C). Prepare 6 muffin cups with cooking spray.

2
Beat quinoa, eggs, feta cheese, mushrooms, onion, thyme, salt, and pepper together in a large bowl. Spoon into prepared muffin cups to about halfway full.

3
Bake in the preheated oven until edges brown and the tops are firm to the touch, 20 to 30 minutes.

NUTRITION FACTS:

94 calories; protein 5.6g; carbohydrates 7.8g; fat 4.5g; cholesterol 98.6mg; sodium 133.3mg.

STUFFED PEPPERS

Prep:
20 **mins**
Cook:
50 **mins**
Total:
70 **mins**
Servings:
4
Yield:
4 **stuffed peppers**

INGREDIENTS:

cooking spray
1 ½ **pounds ground sirloin**
½ **pound bulk pork sausage**
6 **Roma tomatoes, chopped, divided**
1 **small white onion, finely diced**
1 **tablespoon butter**
2 **teaspoons crushed garlic**
1 **teaspoon dried oregano, or to taste**
½ **teaspoon fennel seed, or to taste**
seasoned pepper to taste
4 **large green bell peppers, tops and seeds removed**
6 **ounces crumbled feta cheese**
½ **cup grated Parmesan cheese**
½ **cup shredded mozzarella cheese**

DIRECTIONS:

1

Coat a casserole dish with cooking spray.

2

Cook ground sirloin and sausage in a skillet over medium-low heat until browned and crumbly, stirring often, 5 to 10 minutes. Drain thoroughly. Mix in 3/4 the tomatoes, onion, butter, garlic, oregano, fennel seed, and seasoned pepper. Simmer over low heat until meat mixture comes together, about 20 minutes.

3

Preheat the oven to 350 degrees F (175 degrees C).

4

Fill bell peppers with meat mixture, alternating with layers of feta cheese and Parmesan cheese. Place stuffed bell peppers side-by-side in the prepared casserole dish; add remaining tomatoes around and under the peppers so they cook up and into the peppers. Sprinkle with mozzarella cheese.

5

Bake in the preheated oven until browned and bubbly, about 30 minutes.

NUTRITION FACTS:

606 calories; protein 54.4g; carbohydrates 17g; fat 35.7g; cholesterol 154.1mg; sodium 1315.3mg.

KETO CHEESE TACO SHELLS

Prep:
10 **mins**
Cook:
6 **mins**
Additional:
12 **mins**
Total:
28 **mins**
Servings:
4
Yield:
4 **taco shells**

INGREDIENTS:

2 **cups shredded Cheddar cheese**

DIRECTIONS:

1
Preheat oven to 400 degrees F (200 degrees C). Line 2 baking sheets with parchment paper or silicone mats.

2
Wrap the handle of a wooden spoon with aluminum foil. Balance between 2 tall cans.

3
Spread Cheddar cheese on the prepared baking sheets into four 6-inch circles placed 2 inches apart.

4
Bake in the preheated oven until cheese melts and is lightly brown, 6 to 8 minutes. Cool for 2 to 3 minutes. Lift with a spatula and drape over the wrapped wooden handle; cool until set, about 10 minutes.

NUTRITION FACTS:

228 **calories;** protein 14.1g; **carbohydrates** 0.7g; **fat** 18.7g; **cholesterol** 59.3mg; **sodium** 350.9mg.

HOT DOG AND DIPPING SAUCE

Prep:
5 **mins**
Total:
5 **mins**
Servings:
1
Yield:
1 serving

INGREDIENTS:

1 tablespoon mayonnaise
1 tablespoon prepared yellow mustard

DIRECTIONS:

Mix mayonnaise and mustard together thoroughly in small bowl.

NUTRITION FACTS:

109 **calories**; **protein** 0.8g; **carbohydrates** 1.3g; **fat** 11.6g; **cholesterol** 5.2mg; **sodium** 253.4mg.

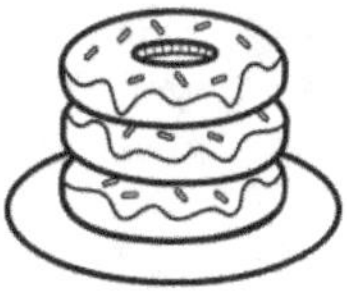

www.ingramcontent.com/pod-product-compliance
Lightning Source LLC
Chambersburg PA
CBHW070934080526
44589CB00013B/1512